ONE LOVED A SOLDIER ANOTHER A SAILOR A THIRD A MARINE

— A MURDER MYSTERY —

Seventh Book in the Zuma Mystery Series

JEROME RABOW, PH.D.

ISBN 978-1-955156-74-5 (paperback)
ISBN 978-1-955156-75-2 (digital)

Copyright © 2021 by Jerome Rabow, Ph.D.

All rights reserved. No part of this publication may be reproduced, distributed, or transmitted in any form or by any means, including photocopying, recording, or other electronic or mechanical methods without the prior written permission of the publisher. For permission requests, solicit the publisher via the address below.

Rushmore Press LLC
1 800 460 9188
www.rushmorepress.com

Printed in the United States of America

TABLE OF CONTENTS

Chapter 1:   The Tides 5
Chapter 2:   Interracial Dating 11
Chapter 3:   Propinquity and Robberies 16
Chapter 4:   The Media and Music 21
Chapter 5:   Blondes and Fords 26
Chapter 6:   Ford Sisters and Andrew Sisters 31
Chapter 7:   Race Doesn't Seem to Matter 37
Chapter 8:   After the Rain the Fires Ain't Out 42

CHAPTER 1

The Tides

Detective Joe Zuma loved getting up with the sun rising and reflecting on the pacific shores of Santa Monica as he walked at the edge of the gentle waves. He compared himself to the tides. If it was low tide, the ocean had washed up the debris, and if it was high, it was cleaned away. It would never stop ... and he thought his work in cleaning up the city of crime would also never stop. It was low tide, and the sun had cleared the bluffs of the palisades so that the ocean now was light grey instead of the dark blue that he had started with. He had been gazing towards the west when he stumbled upon two corpses hat had been washed up.

They were not badly decayed so he could see that one male was Black and the other Latino. There were bullets that had entered the back of their heads. He immediately called the coroner's office to pick up the bodies, and while he was waiting, he checked to see if there were any identifications. He found none. He told the ambulance personnel to call him as soon as they could get an ID and resumed his walk. A tin can was in front of his right foot; he kicked it and thought of Randy Newman's lyrics:

"Tin can at my feet, / Kick it down the street / That's no way to treat a friend."

Zuma thought, *Indeed, that's no way to treat a friend.*

Zuma headed home, took a shower, and saw his wife Claudia. She was not awake yet, and he saw that she had set the alarm for eight thirty, so he set the coffee machine to start its drip process at that time, kissed her gently on the cheek, and left for the office.

When Zuma got to the office, there were reports of some minor theft at a few all-night shops on his desk. The owners had reported kids walking in and stealing food, candy, and beer. He sent two of his officers out to investigate. Those thefts usually resulted in no apprehensions. The kids came from different neighborhoods so the owners had never recognized them before.

The two corpses bothered him. It was unusual for a Black and a Latino person to have been killed while they were together. He called in his new associate, Detective Zack Phillips. Phillips had replaced his long-time colleague and partner Pat Vasquez who left and was now head of the Los Angeles Police Department.

"Zack, while were waiting for some identifications what would your theories be about a Black and a Latino man being murdered?"

"They could have been lovers. Homophobia is still rampant, and it would be especially galling to any homophobe to see a mixed racial couple."

Zuma like it that Zack saw political implications in many of the crimes. He was a political science major at UCLA and graduated at the top of the Police Academy.

"Why not just shoot them? Why dump them in the ocean?"

"Don't know, Joe. A second theory would be the income inequality that exists in our community. Rich folks just don't like seeing what they assume to be poor folks walking in their community. But if that were true, it still would not explain the dumping in the ocean."

"Any others?"

"Maybe some gang kids got in trouble with their gangs for scheming or because they were lovers. Gangs would dump anyone in the ocean they thought was a threat as a way to warn others in the gang."

"I like it, Zack, that you can deal in street-level politics as well as grander theories. I guess we'll wait to see what the coroner finds about these two men. Zack, could you check on the guys I sent out to investigate those robberies? Nothing else is pressing so I think I am going to try and meet Claudia for lunch."

Zuma made sure to punch out so that the department would be not paying for his personal time. It was not often that he could take off in the middle of a day.

He felt lucky and blessed to have Claudia who brought passion to her love for him and whose work as a painter of landscapes contrasted so sharply to his daily life of dealing with murderers. She also worked at a local school and was mentoring students who were interestd in painting. She did not charge them, and it was on her own time. They were each in a second marriage, and felt lucky and blessed that things seemed to be going very well. Zuma had lost his first wife to a hit-and-run incident. Claudia realized shortly after she had married the first time that the guy was no good, but it took her a while to get rid of him.

When Zuma got back to the office, Zack told him that the coroner had not been able to track any criminal records of the fingerprints. He would hold onto the bodies with the possibility that a next of kin would report a missing relative. Zuma confirmed this, saying, "It usually takes three days before we accept a missing person's report. Since it's already been a day, we might hear from someone by the end of the week." Zack also said that each of the two owners said that it was a group of four kids who seemed to be Black and Brown.

Zack who had a background in juvenile crime said that gangs, in their efforts to recruit members, will send them out on small things like the robbery that was committed in order to discover who handled themselves well. This could be why the robbery was committed.

"But it wouldn't explain the multi-racial mix of the kids. I don't get that."

Zuma liked that Zack was able to say that he did not have all the answers.

"I wonder if there could be a connection between the multi-racial couple whose bodies he had discovered and the multi-racial robberes."

"You have taught me to assume that there are no concidences."

"Let's hope we get the missing person's reports. I'll see you tomorrow morning."

On the next day, in his early morning run, he did not have the opportunity to stumble upon corpses because a crowd had already gathered around the bodies. When Zuma got close, he saw it was a male and female—an interracial couple that had been shot. He assumed it would be the same MO with no ID, but he was wrong. The driver's license of each was there so the murderer obviously wanted the police to know who it was and notify the next of kin. He smiled as he thought about Zack's comments about no concidences, but he was deeply concerned and puzzled about all the interracial activites that had transpired in the past two days.

"Zack, we're going to have to pay a vist to the addresses listed on the driver's license. Do you want to take one, and I'll take the other?"

"No. I prefer we do both of them together."

The kin of the white female who was found shot opened the door; Zuma and Zack were greeeted by a white couple, who identified themselves as Mr. and Mrs. Ducat. After establishing that they had not heard from their daughter, Zuma spoke.

"I regret to give you the sad news that your daughter was found on the beach. She had been shot." Zuma waited to see if they were going to ask any questions. "You will have to go down to the morgue to confirm it was your daugheter. I assume you will also want to give her a funeral."

"Oh god, I knew that dating a Black man would get her in trouble. We are not against it, but I know many people in this community don't like it. We were always worried for her safety."

"Did you know the man she was dating?"

"No, she talked about him and seemed very much in love. But we never met him."

A Black male was also shot and found next to your daughter. Presumably, he was the man your daugher was in love with. His name was Edward Jackson. Again, we are sorry for your loss, but if you have any idea of who would want to hurt your daughter or Mr. Jackson, please get in touch with us."

The kin to Edward Jackson, a Black couple who identified themselvs his parents, told their story, and it sounded very similar to what the Ducats had said. Their son was in love. They knew she was white, and they were worried. They had never met the woman. They knew he was going to have a hard time just for being gay and Black, and this would only be compounded if he was with a white person.

"Hopefully, they might remember someone who had gotten angry with their kids and will get back to us. As of now, we have four corpses, two robberies, and no suspects. We will just need to be patient. Let me make a call to Pat Vasquez. He has some special gang units working in the inner city, and he might know something about this new brand of interracial cooperation between rival gangs."

"Joe, we have some new information on the gangs' cooooperative efforts. It seems like their informal truce not to invade the others' territory for drug selling was broken by some of the rival gangs just shooting each other. The leaders felt this would lead to a crackdown, so they decided to do something about decreasing hostilities."

"That's unbelievable, Pat. Gangs doing diversity training."

"Yeah, and they are going about it by sending teams into neighborhoods to convince them they can work together, and when they go back to their respective gangs, they can arbitrate hostilities."

"That's the model all corporations use."

"Yeah, these gang leaders are pretty savvy gangsters. They would have had high GPAs in college."

"They still have high GPAs. But now it doesn't stand for Grade Point Average but for Gang Potential Allegiance."

Zuma knew that given different opportunities, these gang leaders—who needed intellectual and emotional intelligence to run a gang—would be heads of corporations.

"Pat, do you have any plans to do anything?"

"No, I think if I just leave it alone, it might reduce murders in my community even though it would not change the robbery rates in your community."

"Pat, would you be adverse to infiltrating the two gangs in order to find out when they're sending out their recuts to the robberies? I'm not sure exactly how this would work, but it might help us."

"I'll get on it right away, Joe. Nothing to lose."

Chapter 2

Interracial Dating

The Ducats called and told Zuma they had remembered that someone at her work had made dispariging remarks about interracial dating. Joe got the number and decided that he and Zack would visit the organization. It was a nonprofit designed to help battered women. Zuma couldn't imagine why anyone working in such an oragnization would be opposed to interracial dating. Most of the women who were in the shelters the organization provided had experiences in interracial relationships. On their way over the coroner's office called and said there was nothing they could find on the books about the two men who Zuma had discovered on the beach.

"Zack, we're just going to have to wait 'til someone reports a missing family member. Do you want to take the lead on questions to the shelter staff?"

"Sure, Joe."

Zack's questioning of the staff that worked with the Ducats' daughter all reported that she was a gentle soul. She had acknowledged to them that she was in love and was planning to move in with her boyfriend. None of the women seemed upset that the boyfriend was Black, but when many indicated to her that interracial couples had a difficult time in this city, she had said that if it gets too dificult, they would move to a friendly city like Berkeley.

The questions of the staff where Edward Jackson worked revealed a similar portrait of a person very much in love but was aware of the dfficulties that lay ahead and was flexible about moving, even if it meant leaving his family.

"Too bad, Joe. I think of them now as star struck lovers, and despite all their awareness still gunned down by the hatreds that abound in our society."

"Yes, Zack. There is a song that fits this situaton. I know the one by Billy Joel, and the title is 'Only the Good Die Young.'"

Zack, who had played classical music on the piano as a child but now only listened to jazz, loved the introduction to popular music that Zuma was bringing into his life.

"I'll definitely check that one out, Joe. Thank you."

"I'm going home now, Zack. I'm still a starstruck lover, and I believe it will last for many years to come."

"I'm hoping that will also happen to me, Joe."

"Zack, love is similar to solving solving crimes."

"How's that, Joe?"

"They both require patience."

"I got tons of patience for crimes, Joe, just don't have it for life. Any suggestions?"

"Practice. Practice. Practice. When you're standing in a long line at the market, or you can't get the seat you want at the movie—that's when you practice acceptance."

On the way home, Zuma got a call from Pat saying the robberies were going to take place that night. He called Zack.

"Zack, the gang kids are coming in tonight. They will be getting into town around eleven or so. Call every market that sells beer and is open after ten and tell them to be on alert for an interracial group of three or four kids. They are to do nothing except call the number you give them. Make sure they are not going to do anything to alert the kids. We can have three squad cars on the alert throughout Santa Monica and be at the store in two minutes. Do you think those logistics can be managed?"

"Absolutely, Joe. I will wait for the kids to be brought in and will hold them until the morning."

"I need to call Pat and tell him that we are going to bust the kids and that the undercover guy needs to get out. As the new kid on the block, the gang leaders will be most suspicious of him."

Two calls came in from separate markets. The squad car arrived in time to corner the kids from one market, with their stolen good. The second market call came in but the kids had left. The owner had made a fuss about what the kids were doing, and they fled. He called, but it was too late.

When Zuma arrived in the morning, Zack told him the three kids had been held in a cell. They were scared and did not know they could call a lawyer. Appparently, they callled their parents. Zuma also had a message marked urgent to call Pat.

"Joe, the gang is holding my undercover agent. They are threatening to do something to him unless I agree to their demands."

"What do they want? I assume they want the kids released."

"No. I don't think they give a damn about those kids. They want me to promise theat there will be no more efforts to infilatrate their membertship. We had an agreement they would not shoot police officers or citizens ass long as we would let them make sales and only pick up the buyers. I broke it, and they are threatening to go all out on officers. I don't want that to happen."

"Of course not. Make your promise. Do you think you can ask them to stop their robberies?"

"I can ask, but that is the way they recurit. I can't imagine they will agree."

The parents of each of the three boys turned up by the afternoon. Zuma and Zack put them all one room.

"Detective Phillips and I would prefer not to press charges so that none of you would get a juvenile record. In exchange for that, you need to show the homework you have done each week to your parents, and you need to show us that you are not missing any days at school. Is that clear, and is it acceptable?"

"I can't speak for the other parents, but I find your terms very generous and fair. I will make sure we see his homework and that he shows you his attendance record. I want to thank both of you."

The two other sets of parents agreed to the terms and were also appreciative of the offer that Zuma had made to the kids.

"Joe, I esatblished our former agreement for peaceful co-existence, and they are releasing my guy. But they woul not budge on the issue of further robberies."

"Pat, I'm worried what might happen to the kids we released. The gang may want to show potential recruits what might happen if they don't follow strict orders. Can you put some security on the three kids' homes? I can give you the addresses. Meanwhile, we can keep squad cars in the city to monitor the stores as they are not going to stop robberies."

"They might do them in other cities, Joe."

"I understand that that is a possibility. And I'm wondering why they keep training these kids exclusively in Santa Monica. If you have any ideas on that, Pat, please let me know."

"I don't know, Joe. Culver City is just as close. Do you think they have acess to someone in your department, and if so, how would that help them?"

"I think the answer to that question is going to require us to be patient."

The gang was waiting for each of the kids to return to their homes, and each one of the kids was shot in front of their parents.

Zuma got that information and became very upset. He knew that releasing the kids would put them in jeopardy, and that was why he had asked Pat to give them some protection but hadn't thought the gang would be waiting for their arrival. Maybe there was someone in his department who was working closely with the gangs. And how would he and Zack go about trying to figure out who it might be? He knew that this would prove to be a test of his and Zack's patience.

CHAPTER 3

Propinquity and Robberies

The funerals for the three kids were attended by Zuma, Pat, Zack, and gang leaders, as well as members from each of the two gangs. It was a remarkable scene with Zuma and Zack being the only whites in attendance in the all Black and Brown crowd. Zuma knew that the gangs were not in mourning but were there to make a statement to the community and to future applicants. The statement was, "You need to be ambitious to join."

The proof that the gangs were not in mourning came that evening when two more robberies occured. Both were sucessful. There had been no squad cars set up.

"Zack, we've got four corpses from the beach with no clues, three from the inner city knowing who was responsible, and a possible insider working with the gangs."

"Yeah, Joe, this is a test of my patience on crime. I do have another thought about why the gangs keep coming to Santa Monica and not Culver City. Culver is too upscale, and the kids would stand out the moment their car pulled up and they got out. And we are not as upscale as Culver City has become. We have a lot more homeless and vagrants. The kids would not stand out."

"That sounds reasonable. Any othe theories?"

"It is not convenient to get back on the freeway from Culver. Robbers need to get away as quickly as possible. Our town lends itself to easy acess off and speedy return to the freeway."

"That may explain why I think there is an insider. I'll concede that I could be wrong. That still leaves us with seven dead people."

The call came to Zuma who quicly turned to Zack.

"I'm wrong again, Zack. We ve got nine corpses now. A couple was just shot at the mall. The officers say it was Mr. and Mrs. Ducat."

"They were the parents of the girl whose body we found on the beach, Joe."

"Not that it matters, Zack, but that's our first murder not involving an interracial couple. Both of the Ducats were white."

"Joe, maybe it does matteer. Someone not liking the parents of a white girl dating interracially may not like the parents of a Black son who also dares to date interracially. I think we'd better hurry and warn the Jacksons. They are probably in danger and need to be extra cautious."

When Zuma and Zack arrived at the Jackson residence, a crowd is on the steps. They knew immmediately that they were too late. The neighbors came out when they heard gun shots, and the Jacksons were in the doorway on the floor. They had both been shot. No one saw who did it; they saw a car speeding away but no one was able to get a plate.

"I'm willing to bet the caliber of the gun used was the same as the one used on the Ducats."

"I'm sure you're right, Zack. What a field day the media are going to have with this. Four dead with just a couple of hours. The headlines will be screaming about Santa Monica becoming the murder capital of California."

"It does look bad. We have eight bodies and no clues. Plus the three kids from Pat's district. It's not too difficult to see why the media would be alarmed. Joe, this is really going to test our patience."

The bullets that killed the Ducats and the Jacksons matched each other. The crime lab said the weapon that fired the gun belonged to a Mr. Rex Ford. They got an address, and on the way over, Zuma excitedly said that this was the first clue in the case.

Mr. Rex Ford was white, tall, and buit like an ox. You could sense immediately that he was not afraid of fighting anyone and would be eager to do so.

"Mr. Ford, we are aware that you own a Glock 38. Would you be willing to show it to us? Can you tell us the last time you used it?"

"Unless you have a warrant, I don't have to show you nothin', and I don't have to answer any of your goddamn questions. So, now, get the hell off my property."

"Mr. Ford, we can easily get a warrant. Bullets that were found on four bodies came from a weapon registered to you. We can bring you down for suspicion of murder right now, but we just thought we could check your weapon to see if it had been fired recently. If it hasn't, we would just let you go. But if you don't want to cooperate, that's your choice."

"You bet it's my choice. We still got a few choices left in this country. I'll make another choice right now to call my lawyer, and you can haul me in."

Zuma recognized the lawyer as a top criminal defender from an expensive downtown law firm. His name was Melvin Oliver.

"Rex, you're going to have to show them the weapon. The caliber on the bullets show it's registered to you. They could easily get a warrant. If they do that, you know they're going to tear your place upside down."

"I don't give a shit what they do. They won't believe me no matter what I say. They won't find any goddamn weapon, and I can provide an alibi for where I was at the time of the two shootings."

Zuma spotted the lie immediately. He had mentioned four bodies not two separate shootings. Ford had clearly been involved and perhaps had done both shootings, and it was his job to prove it.

"So where were you at the times of the two shootings?"

"Rex, I'd advise you not to answer any questions."

"I ain't got nothin' to be afraid of. I was shooting pool with my buddies."

"And what time was that? And would you give us the names of your buddies?"

"I was shooting pool from one to four, and I'll write down the phone number of the two guys I was playing pool with."

Zuma knew that he was covering his butt by indicating the hours of pool playing. That was the times the two couple had been murdered. He also was sure his buddies would vouch for him.

"And tell us the pool hall that you were playing in."

Ford knew he would be caught unless he got to the owner of the pool parlor before Zuma did.

"I'm not sure. I have the place written down. My buddy picked it out. When I get back, I'll call you."

Ford did call in a number, and Zack and Zuma headed over to the parlor. The owner said he did not recognize the name but did recognize the mug shot of Ford.

"If you are lying to us, sir, you will go to jail for conspiring to protect a possible murderer, and you will lose your license."

"Both of those are better than the alternative, which is him murdering me. I've told you all I could. This way, I'll stay alive."

Zuma knew that Ford's buddies would be of no more help than the pool owner.

"This guy is something. He seems very confident that he's covered all his bases. Let's get the warrant and tear the goddamn place up."

When the returned to Ford's home they found the address of the Ducats and the Jacksons on a pad. They also found a lot of Aryan, pro-Nazi type pamphlets about the dangers of mingling the races.

"Let's bust this wise guy and book him on suspicion of murder. We'll see how much he can afford to spend on his fancy criminal defense lawyer."

Even as he spoke these words Zuma knew that a trial would not lead to a conviction. They had no weapon and no witnesses.

"He got us, Zack. It may cost him a few bucks, but we're not going to get a conviction, unless we can get a witness to the shooting or at least find the weapon."

CHAPTER 4

The Media and Music

There was an enormous crowd in front of the precinct—media personnel recording everything, the public carrying signs about needing more protection, and sympathizers saying freedom of choice needs to be protected in America. They also had a soundtrack that was playing—the Tom Petty song "I Won't Back Down." Zuma loved that song and laughed at how it was being misused. He doubted it would make Petty or anyone else in his famous group "Tom Petty and The Heartbreakers" happy to see who was using it.

A break in the case came when one of the men in his daily collection of garbage noticed that a weapon was in the trash that he was dumping at the local dumpsite. He had called in to his boss to ask if he could keep it, but the boss said that it had to be turned over since it was a possible murder weapon. It would do the garbage collector more harm if he ever used it, and he would have a lot of explaining to do.

Ford testified that he had no idea how his weapon had ended up in a garbage truck. He hadn't used it in a year so maybe it had been stolen. His case was not going to win the sympathy of the jurors, some of whom were Black and Latino. Upon going home at night, they saw on TV the all-white demonstrators carrying pro-Nazi flags. Zuma knew there might be a conviction but probably not for murder.

It did not take the jury, mostly Latinos and Blacks, a long time to come back with a conviction. However, the judge said that there were no witnesses, and since there were no fingerprints on the gun, he could not go along with the jury's decision for a conviction. He scolded the jurors for not relying on evidence.

The communities of color protested vehemently against the judges' decision while Ford's sympathizers hailed it as a victory for their cause of freedom and free speech.

Throughout his career, Zuma had never felt unable to figure out where to go next. There was always something that might be done to move forward in the solution of a crime. This was not one of those times.

"Zack, I'd like you to handle the media. Tell them that we might have some new clues, and maybe they'll get off our backs. If you want to address the public though TV, assure them that this is not the work of a raving maniac but someone who carefully selects his targets. They should all be extra careful and call in any suspicious activity, especially if they feel that they are being followed. I'm going to have to have a quiet dinner with Claudia. You can join us if you'd like."

"Thanks, Joe, I don't know how long the media stuff will last, and I also need some quiet. I'll just plan on seeing you in the morning."

Claudia knew that Joe would be under stress as she had seen the TV, and so, she prepared Zuma's favorite dinner: salmon and whole wheat pasta. When they finished diner, they turned on the TV and saw that Zack had been asked if Detective Zuma was considering resigning.

"I can't speak for Detective Zuma. You should be asking him that question. But you should not even be asking that question about someone who has served this city so well. I certainly hope he doesn't, and knowing him as I do, I don't think that such a thing has entered his mind. Detective Zuma is not a quitter."

Claudia and Zuma were proud of the way Zack had fielded the question and were pleased with his endorsement of his character.

"You are anything but a quitter, darling, and I know you will figure this whole mess out. You always do. I have complete confidence in you. I know you, and so does Zack. Let's go to bed now. Tomorrow will be a better day."

On his early morning walk, Zuma saw two of the homeless men, whom he had always seen on his walks, approaching him.

"Detective, we'd like to speak with you. You have always been fair with us, and when we heard that there was talk about your resignation, the men agreed we would not like to see that. They would bring in some hard-ass who hates the homeless and who would start to really kick us around. We want to give you some information that we would ordinarily keep quiet about."

Zuma waited.

"We saw a woman shoot the two couples. It was the same woman."

"Wow, thank you. What else can you tell me about her? Color? Height? Age?"

"She was white, on the biggish side, and may have been about fifty years old. She did not have any grey hair so she could have easily been younger."

"Are you pretty sure? It was late in the day, and probably close to dark. Could you see that well? Would you be able to recognize her again?"

"Absolutely, Detective. She turned and saw us and ignored us as if we were not human beings who would every dare say anything."

"Thank you, gentlemen. I appreciate your help and your support for my handling of the homeless situation."

On the way back home to shower and prepare for work, Zuma began thinking about who might be under or about fifty years old and related to any of the people that were involved in the case. It would have to be a strong and confident woman. By the time he pulled up to the precinct, he was singing some of the lyrics to the Chaka Kahn version of "I'm Every Woman":

> It's all in me
> Anything you want done, baby,
> I'll do it naturally
> I'm every woman,
> It's all in me
> Anytime you feel danger or fear,
> Then instantly
> I will appear.

He entered the office smiling, knowing that it would be possible for him to figure out who the woman was.

Zuma told Zack the description that the homeless men had given to him.

"If she was under fifty, that would eliminate the Ducats' mother as well as the Jacksons."

"We're thinking alike, Zack. That leaves only one possibility and that would be our Mrs. Rex Ford. He's twenty-eight, and she could easily be under fifty. She was described as biggish, and that would be similar to his body type."

"Let's figure out where Mrs. Ford lives and see if we can break up this loving mother-son relationship."

"Joe. I've heard of old Fords getting rusty but never heard of one being referred to as middle aged."

"Maybe we can help her age quickly."

The search for a Mrs. Ford in the phone book had six names. One of them, F.R Ford, was assumed to be the best bet since they imagined that she had named her son Rex with something close to her middle name. When they realized where she lived, they felt confident that she was the right woman because it was close to the Ducats' and the Jacksons' apartments.

Upon knocking, they were greeted by a large woman who fit the age and body type description. The woman was as hostile as her son. When Zuma asked if she could account for her whereabouts at a certain hour.

She refused to say anything.

"Have you ever gone to Santa Monica beach?"

"I never go to that goddamn shithole. It's full of hoboes and winos and fleas. I hate them people. They should all be shot."

"We have witnesses who say that you were there."

"Your witnesses are lying; I never go there. What time did they say they saw me?"

"They said it was early evening."

"That's the time I play bridge with my three neighbors. Here are their numbers. Go check with them right now. I'll stand here and won't use my phone to alert them. Keep you stooge with me. You don't think I will get them to lie. You ain't got nothing on me. So just get out. If you come back, I'm going to sue you for harassing me since you don't have one bit of goddamn evidence. I wasn't on any goddamn beach."

"One more question before we leave. Do you know any of your neighbors with the name of Ducat or Jackson?"

"If I did, I wouldn't tell you anything. I keep to myself. Just go to the three friends I play bridge with."

"Joe, she was not in the least worried or intimidated. I tend to think she is telling the truth."

"It felt that way to me also. Let's go back and visit all the other Fords from the phone book."

None of the other Fords resembled the homeless people's descriptions, and all of them seemed like very conventional citizens.

"I don't like that first one, Ford. She may not have committed the murders and may indeed be innocent of that, but she might in some way be linked to the case. She had no reason to be that belligerent. Let's put a tail in front of her home and follow her for the next few days."

CHAPTER 5

Blondes and Fords

"Joe, I tailed the gal after she left her place, and she went into a hair salon. When she came out, she was blonde."

"No need to tell me about her choice of a new hair color, is there, Zack?"

"You're right; that's not important. But two minutes after she returned to the apartment, the same looking woman, height and body build exactly the same, came down but this time she had brown hair. What do you make of that?"

"I doubt if she washed out the coloring. The only other possibility is that there is a twin. Follow her, and we'll get someone in front of the building in case the blonde comes out."

"I will follow her. That's a good suggestion since she was carrying a purse unlike the first one. It appeared stuffed."

The brown-haired woman entered her car, drove away, and got out in front of Rex Ford's apartment. The tail waited, and in fifteen minutes, the woman left. Her purse looked much lighter.

Zuma and Zack got to the blonde's apartment just as she was descending the step. She appeared to be very close to the description that had been provided by the homeless. But this time, the woman had red hair.

Both Zuma and Zack were speechless and just looked at each other.

"I'm glad you're here, Zack, because I would have trouble believing what I saw. Are you thinking what I'm thinking?"

"If you are thinking that the woman just washed out her blonde rinse, and it was red all long, then you're not thinking what I am. What I'm thinking is that we have triplets. We have three female model Fords to go along with our one male model."

"That would explain why the woman was so cocky about her not being involved in any murder and why she could swear that the homeless had been wrong. She never was there. She was covering for one of the other sisters."

"This is a tough one, Zack. They seem like identical triplets. They clearly can cover and lie for each other. What do you see we can do?"

"The major things that differentiates them, aside from the damn hair color, is that one of them is the mother of Rex Ford. We've got to figure out a way to use that connection. He's probably the only person in the whole word who will be able to tell which one is his mother."

"We need to get the triplets in one room and put Rex behind a one-way mirror and wire him up so we can monitor his galvanic skin response. He should have the same responses to his two aunts and a different one to his mother. Their bond is different."

"And what will be able to do with that information?"

"I have no idea, but it's a bit more information than we have now. We will probably figure out a way to use that information, and it's certainly better than what we have now."

By knocking on the door late at night and assuming that they would all be there, they were able to get the three women downtown as possible suspects in a murder investigation.

They hauled Rex in to identify murder suspects. Rex was startled when he saw the three women. After they were all taken out, they were brought in, one at a time and his responses were recorded. It was easy for them to see the differences in his responses to the three women as two of them were the same. Two of the sisters were sent home. The brown-haired Ford was left.

"Rex, I don't think you need any introductions, but just to make sure, this is your mother. Mrs. Ford, I have no doubt you are happy to see your son. Is there a Mr. Ford so that we can possibly have a family reunion?"

Mother and son were unresponsive to the comments and sarcasm of Zuma.

"So, this is what is going to happen. We are going to charge your mom with murder. She will go on trial. It will be easy to get a conviction of some sort since we have witnesses who saw your mom at the time and place of the murders."

"But you ain't got motive and you ain't got a weapon. I'll take my chances and bet she doesn't get a stiff sentence."

"And we are going to look into your two aunts. We've got their fingerprints, and I'm sure they've been involved with something that is illegal. The Ford family does not have unrighteous citizens. You might be the only one who doesn't go to jail, or perhaps, all the Fords will be locked up. And when you do get out, since the papers will have made hay because it would such a good story describing an entire family of criminals, your lives will never be free."

Zuma had registered Rex's comments about taking his chances. He was more than ever convinced that Rex Ford was guilty of more than one thing.

There was no stiff sentence. In fact, there was no sentence at all. On the first day of the trial, another couple, this time they were females were found dead on the beach. The Ford lawyer called for an immediate suspension of the trial since his client could not have been involved. The police were harassing the Ford family. Since there was no weapon, no motive, and only the testimony of two homeless men, the judge concurred, and Mrs. Ford was set free.

Zuma went looking for the homeless men who had helped him out earlier. They were again helpful. This time, the saw a male shooting the female couple. They heard him scream, "Die you fuckin' dykes." They indicated he was well built and about five foot ten inches.

It had to be Rex Ford. But how could that be? The tail at his home reported that he had never left his apartment. Was there a father?

The homeless men did not say the shooter was older.

"What do you make of this new twist, Zack?"

"It would be crazy if there was another twin. The only other thing I can think of is one of the aunts having a son, so the shooter would be our guy's cousin."

"Good thinking. Let's go find this new SOB."

The tails at the sister's apartment were instructed to follow every sister who left. At no time was a sister to be able to go off without being followed. The first few days were fruitless. There were trips to the market and to the park to walk the dog and even walks on the beach where the threesome would get stares from folks who could not believe their eyes. On the fourth day, one of the sisters drove to Culver City. When she parked, a man looking exactly like Rex Ford came out of his apartment and entered her vehicle.

"Let's pick him up and drag him in."

"I think we'd be better off waiting to see where they go."

The woman drove back to where the three sisters lived, and both of them went upstairs.

"I think we can pick him up now. Keep your eye out, Zack, for which one of the sisters gets the most upset."

It was easy to see which sister got most upset as she was the only one who protested the arrest. When she was also told they had eye witnesses, she started laughing and screaming."

"Yeah, yeah, just like your last turkeys. When are you guys going to stop harassing us? Why do you want to go through all this shit again and get no verdict? Stop bothering us and wasting our time and yours."

CHAPTER 6

Ford Sisters and Andrew Sisters

Zuma knew that the case for conviction was as weak as the other. He had nothing he was sure would get a conviction on Rex Ford or his cousin. He felt his only hope was to keep track of the three sisters. If he could find something that would get a conviction and get them locked up, Rex would be alone and might not like seeing his mother or maybe even his aunts in jail.

"Zack, we need to make sure that the three sisters don't go anywhere without being followed. I think of them as our only hope now. I don't care how many tails we have to use or the costs to the department—it has to be twenty-four seven."

Zuma started humming and then began singing. Zack was surprised as Zuma had not sounded happy about his only hope.

> There were three little sisters.
> Three little sisters.
> And each one only in her teens.
> One loved a soldier.
> One loved a sailor.
> And one loved a lad from the marines.

"Joe, you must have pulled that one out of your hat."

"It's an oldie, Zack. Sung by the Andrew sisters who actually were three sisters. Here's the rest of it:

And when the boys marched away,
The girls said they'd be true until the boys marched back
someday.
Now, the three little sisters,
Stay home, home and read their magazines.
You can tell it to the soldier.
Tell it to the sailor.
Ooh, and tell it to the marine.

"I have no idea why I'm singing it, Zack. It's so unusual to find triplets, and on top of that, they are identical. I guess my only hope is still hope. Maybe that's where the song comes from. It's a nice little ditty about loyalty and love."

"It also applies to the sisters, Joe, with their tremendous loyalty to each other. It actually applies to the whole bloody clan of Fords."

The three sisters waited for two days, and in the dead of night, they piled into a station wagon and headed south on the 405.

"This reminds me of the good old days when we were younger and were all together in a car. That was really fun."

"Maybe they were good for you, but not for me."

"What do you mean? Why not?"

"I was just polite trying to be right. If I wasn't, you, my dear boss Betty, were always petty. And Tina was a dancing ballerina."

"Being the youngest, I never got mentioned. I had to dance trying to get your attention."

"Well, we're together again, and it still feels like fun to me, and I'm still the boss, so we need to get ready to cross the border. Make sure you have your seatbelts on and passports ready."

When it was clear that they were going to cross the border, Zuma knew it was useless to alert the Mexican police, so he instructed the two men in the on car to do as best as they could to follow them. The women crossed into Mexico and waved at the guards who seemed to know them. They pulled into a motel, and in ten minutes, they each came out but went separate ways with only one taking the wagon and the other two walking in the opposite direction.

"I'll use the car to follow her. We're probably going to lose one, but that's the best we can do."

The two walkers split up after five minutes each taking a different road. The car parked after only five minutes, and the woman got out and entered a motel. If there could be a camera that was observing the three women, it would record that they all came out carrying packages. The two detectives only saw two of the women. But when the detectives returned, they saw all three women smiling and carrying their packages.

"Detective Zuma, we're pretty sure the women made a pickup of drugs. Do you want us to stop and arrest them after they go across the border?"

"No, let's wait 'til they get back. To Santa Monica. We need to see what they will do with their packages. Make sure you get a picture of the car crossing the border. That's a big offense if it turns out that you're right about drugs. Good work. Let us know if they go directly back or make stops along the way. Write down any address of their stops. See if they go in with something and come out empty."

Zuma started singing again. Zack had never seen Zuma so exuberant. This time Zack knew the song; it was a Jackson Browne tune, "Running on Empty." Zuma sang the words:

> Looking out at the road rushing under my wheels
> Looking back at the years gone by like so many summer
>   fields
> In sixty-five I was seventeen and running up one-on-one
> I don't know where I'm running now, I'm just running on
> Running on empty
> Running on running blind
> Running on running into the sun.
> But I'm running behind.

"I'm not running behind, Zack, and I'm not running blind. The sun is definitely at my back."

The tails recorded three addresses where the three sisters delivered their packages. The tails knew it was a different sister at each address because of the different hair coloring. Each of the sisters left the address with a new package.

"It's time to act. Get a warrant so we can go to those three addresses. I'm sure there will be drugs. Pick up whatever else you can. Take each of them or as many as are in the place down to the station, and book them on charges of selling drugs. Take their wives and children in if you have to. You'll need more than three men at each address. Let's visit the sisters. We need to look for money and any addresses other than the three we already have. Zack, I think we have the three of them running on empty."

After Zack read them their rights, they asked to make the call to Rex rather than a lawyer. They knew he would call the lawyer, and they wanted him to know so he would be there at the booking.

Zuma hummed all the way to the station as the sisters stared at him. They thought he was something from outer space. Zuma was from outer space. He was flying high, and he wasn't on empty.

Rex Ford and his lawyer were there just as Zuma pulled in with the three sisters.

"What are you planning to charge my clients with, Detective Zuma?"

"We believe they transported drugs illegally into the US."

"Nonsense. They went shopping in Mexico, looking for bargains."

"You may be right. They may have gotten drugs at a bargain price."

"Sure, everyone is always on the hunt for bargains."

"It's pretty strange, don't you think, that for people who don't like Mexicans, they travel to Mexico and then deliver packages to Mexican families? What would they do without Mexicans?"

"Even if you were to find drugs, there is no proof they were transported from Mexico."

"We'll see. Right now, we're inspecting the apartment. My guess is we will find fingerprints on the three bags they carried upstairs. We have pictures of the bags they carried. If the bags match, I'm pretty sure even you would know we have a very good case."

"I need to confer with my clients."

"While you are advising your clients, please tell them we'd like the name of the murderer and any other names of dealers that they sell to. If they provide us with that information, I would recommend a less harsh sentence to the district attorney."

"We can't give up the name, and if we supply other dealer names, we will all be dead very quickly."

"I could set it up so that the newspapers print a story about a drug bust and other valuable information that was found. In that way, it doesn't look like you gave names. That leaves the issue of the murderer."

The sisters all stared at each other and nodded their heads 'no.'

"Please reconsider. They will not require you to testify against a family member. Even if you give them the name of the murderer, they have no weapon and no motive. They just have those hoboes as eyewitnesses, and we have seen how much that's worth. It will not be a strong case against him. They do have a strong case against you. It's your chance to cut years off your sentence."

"Give us a few moments. We need to be alone."

"It's your call, Betty. He's our nephew, but he's your son. Whatever you decide to do, we will back you. We know this has got to be a tough decision."

"If I give up my son, we get lighter sentences, and he runs the risk of a weak trial. If I shut up, we all get heavier sentences, and he is likely to be free. It's not as difficult as you said. I loved my son.

I loved teaching him how to steal things in groceries. He was very creative. I taught him about the brutality of Blacks and the slyness of Mexicans. He had a great reputation in grade school. The Black and Latino kids were afraid of him. When he got older, I liked how he would protect me if anyone looked like they might be eyeing my purse. He always respected me. We loved and admired each other. In fact, it's a no brainer for me. I can't and never will give up my son."

"Detective Zuma, my clients have said all they want to say. You may go ahead with the booking so I can prepare bail money."

Zuma thought it would be better for the case if they were put into one cell. In that way, because they were seeing each other moment after moment, it would really strike two of them that they were going to get a longer sentence because one of them would not sacrifice. The Mexican men who had been booked on charges of possession glared and stared and flipped the sisters off whenever they had the opportunity. The women talked among themselves and felt that their lives might be safer in prison.

Zuma headed home after saying goodbye to Zack. He was feeling good because three drug dealers were going to be out of business for a while, and he was going after more and had a murderer who might be convicted. And three women who sold drugs were also going to be off the streets.

He was recounting his pleasant feelings to Claudia when a call came in that interrupted dinner and put an end to his good feelings. Another couple had been shot on the beach. Zuma apologized to Claudia for having to leave dinner and called Zack.

"Zack, meet me on the beach underneath the pier. We got a brand-new mess on our plate."

CHAPTER 7

Race Doesn't Seem to Matter

A white couple, aged about fifty, had been shot in the back of the head, execution style. The hoboes had been scared away when they saw three men carrying guns walking towards the pier. They were not sure of the race but thought they might be Mexican or white.

"Zack, I don't think Rex Ford would shoot a white couple, and he operates alone, not in a gang."

"If the hoboes were correct about Mexicans, that would make sense Joe. They had been busted by three white women and their fellow dealers were trying to send a message to the women in jail to not testify against the dealers who had been busted."

"Going back to Ford, he would have the motive to suggest that the murders were not racially motivated, and his family was not involved. Zack, I don't think he would have any trouble rounding up some cronies and making up a story convincing them that the white couple was liberal and were campaigning to integrate Santa Monica."

"Let's get back to Ford. Maybe he wasn't so careful about his gun this time, or maybe we can somehow find his cronies while they are all celebrating. Maybe the hoboes were not correct about the race of the shooters."

Ford and two other men were leaving his apartment when Zuma and Zack pulled up. When questioned about their whereabouts last night, they said they were playing cards.

"Why are you harassing us, Detective? We were just going out to have lunch and shoot some pool."

"Another couple was murdered last night."

"As we just said, we were playing cards and were never on the beach."

Ford and Zuma spotted the error right away. How would he know the murder was on the beach? Neither Zuma nor Zack had mentioned that fact. Zuma decided to not follow up the beach issue. There were no witnesses to the shootings. He thought he'd have a better chance to follow up with the card game and to see what else they might be up to.

"Can anyone verify your card playing and the time?"

"No problem, Detective. We sent out for pizza at seven and beer at ten thirty. You can check with the stores or the delivery boys."

Zuma recognized that would still allow them time after they had eaten the pizza to get to the beach and return to order their beer. He decided to say nothing.

"Zack, I know they were there. I don't know how I can prove it, but I know they were at the beach during the time of the shooting."

"Your instincts are usually right, Joe. What do we do now?"

"Let's put a tail on the three comrades and see what they else they might be planning."

The three men headed for the jail where each of them visited one sister. When they conferred afterwards, they all had the same story. The women were scared about being killed in jail by the Mexicans who had been arrested later on when they would be serving their sentences or even when they got out. They felt their lives would be at risk in or out of jail.

"Let's pay the women another visit, but only after we visit some of those dealers. After we do that, we can reassure them they will be safe. The three men, with Rex Ford driving, headed toward the homes of the dealers who had been arrested."

Zuma and Zack waited 'til the men came out.

"Can you tell us what you were speaking to the women about?"

"Sure, detectives. Happy to cooperate. We told them that if anything happened to members of our family, we would make sure that all members of their family would be shot, and even their children's lives would be taken. It took some time for them to realize that their husbands could not protect them. We are now waiting for them to come down so we can drive the women to the jail so they could report the information to their husbands."

"Wasn't that a threat that you made?"

"We see it as information about the facts of life. You know, like the birds and the bees."

The detectives followed the men who drove the women and waited 'til they all emerged. It took a half hour before the men emerged.

"Hi again, detectives. We wanted to make sure the women had communicated the facts of life, and we asked if their husbands understood. They three women said their husbands understood. We're happy to report that the facts of life are now known by all. The hoboes who had been scared away by the shooters showed up at the precinct. They reported that even though they were frightened and ran away, they did see three other men slowly walking towards the couple. The men stopped when they heard the shots and turned around, walking back toward the direction they came from."

"Do you think you could recognize them?"

"No, it was getting dark and they were too far away. The only thing we are sure of was that there were three of them."

"Zack, my instincts were right. They were on the beach. They didn't shoot the couple, but they were there. We could pick them up and hold them for leaving the scene of a crime.

"Seems like there is more serious stuff than the threats and leaving the scene of a crime, Joe. Let's wait. We could always use those if we have to."

"Thanks for your help, gentlemen. Grab some coffee and any other goodies on the table on your way out."

The hoboes stuffed their pockets with everything they could grab. Nothing was left.

In the middle of the night, Zuma received a phone call. The tails reported that three men were in a car heading south and passing San Diego.

"We're being followed. Let's make sure we don't get picked up for anything silly like going too fast or not staying in our goddamn lane. I don't know if they are going to follow us across the border. We need to get past the border."

"Captain Zuma, it looks like they are going to cross the border. What would you like us to do?"

"Follow them as best as you can. I'm sure they know they are being followed. Zack and I will leave right away. We can make it there in under ninety minutes. Keep us posted."

Zuma had the sirens and lights on the entire distance. They had no trouble crossing the border and caught up to the tails who reported that the three men were having lunch and had been in there for two hours, drinking sangria and eating tacos. Zuma knew that this wasn't a lunch stop. This must be where they scored their drugs. The three men came out carrying nothing and headed back into Santa Monica.

"Zack, I think you were right to wait. They probably purchased drugs. The drugs will somehow find their way back. They will pick them up or have them delivered. We have to watch them like a dog on a bone. So far, they have been able to stay one step ahead of us, and it may not only be the best chance we have to nail them and put them away one, but the only one we're going to get for a long time. We can report the possible drug dealer at the taco place to the Mexican police."

It took two days before a very young kid showed up carrying a package. He looked nervous, and Zuma knew he was delivering drugs. They waited until the young kid had entered the apartment. They waited two minutes before breaking down the door and saw the three men weighing the packages of drugs. It was clearly cocaine.

"Hey, kid, get out of here. When you get back, tell your boss we know what he's been up to. Now scram. Vamoose."

Zuma turned to the three men.

"Gentlemen, you have a lot of questions to answer and explaining to do. Here's the phone so you can call your lawyer in case you want to clam up and have him do all the talking for the three of you. Zack, you stay here, take pictures and gather all the evidence you can. Look for other telephone numbers anywhere in the apartment. I'm sure they have other drugs stashed somewhere. A good dealer never runs out of drugs. Don't be afraid to search everything, and don't worry about leaving a mess. Call for some help. I'll meet you back at the precinct."

Chapter 8

After the Rain the Fires Ain't Out

In the car, the toothpick came out of his shirt pocket and Zuma began singing some of the lyrics to "Have You Ever Seen the Rain?":

> I know it's been comin' for some time.
> When it's over so they say
> It'll rain a sunny day.
> I want to know
> have you ever seen the rain?

"Gentlemen, your rainy day is about to arrive."

"Are you planning to book my clients, detective, or entertaining them? What are your grounds for booking them?"

"Oh, let me count. One, leaving the scene of a crime.; two, three pounds of cocaine found in their apartment; three, addresses of known drug dealers that were also found in their home.; four, another pound of cocaine buried in a mattress. We also found a bunch of Aryan magazines with phone numbers of suspected dealers that we are checking on right now. I think I have enough to convince any district attorney that these are not exactly your most upright citizens."

"I don't think my clients appreciate your sarcasm, Detective Zuma, and neither do I."

"Mr. Tabachnick, my sarcasm may be the best thing your clients will have in their lives for the next few years. I'm going to book them and strongly suggest to the district attorney that there be no bail allowed. They clearly are a flight risk."

"Zack, let's put Rex Ford in a cell close to his cousins so they can talk with each other. Let's head back, and see what we've got and see what we can do to wrap up this case. I know we still haven't found the killers of the last couple. We have to file with the district attorney. We also might think about how they might plea."

"We have ten dead, three sisters, and two sons who are cousins in jail and a couple of cronies of one of the sons and a trial."

"Our wall has seventeen pictures on it, Joe. This has been one huge case."

Zuma's phone rang. He picked it up and saw that it was Pat calling him on his private line.

"Joe, the two gang leaders just called and told me they have the people who murdered the white couple on your beach. They were worried that if they were caught, it might lead to attacks on the Mexican community. They asked if I would prefer that they bring them in, or they would take care of them?"

"What did they mean by "take care of them?""

"Joe, you know they always take care of things. The bodies would just disappear, never to be discovered."

"Pat, I don't think you nor I want to be responsible for two murders. Tell them to bring you the men. You can go ahead and charge them since they're in your district. I assume you will get a confession, and they will be put away. Keep it as quiet as you can so there won't be any attacks on the Mexican community. Once you get a confession, let me know so I can indicate on the couple's folder that the case had been solved."

Tabachnick called and asked Joe what he would need from his clients so that the recommendation to the district attorney would be softened.

"Tell me what you are prepared to offer. I can't imagine what it will be."

"They are prepared to give up the nephew."

"We already know it's the nephew. Are you saying they will give testimony in court?"

"No, they do not want to do that."

"I don't think I'm getting anything from you that will make me change my mind when I speak to the district attorney."

"I told them it was a weak offer, but they insisted I try. Thanks, Detective Zuma."

The Ford family could not afford to have their lawyer try each case individually, so they were going to be tried as a whole.

The trial became a showcase for the newspapers. An entire family came into the court every day, dressed in their prison garb. The defense argued circumstantial evidence; no witnesses or weapons had been found. The prosecution laid out all the circumstantial evidence, arguing that when you consider each of those facts, it is something that can't be easily dismissed. The family was also depicted as being sympathetic to Aryan causes, one that despised Mexicans and Blacks.

Newspaper sales skyrocketed. The nightly news had interviews with the public about the family.

The jury brought in a verdict of five years to be served in prison. The judge rejected the verdict and added five more. He also gave a speech that there is no room in America for the kind of hatred that the family expressed. On the way out of the courtroom, Rex Ford leaned over when he passed Zuma and whispered in his ear.

"I've already been offered a book deal for one million bucks. Will be making money while we sit in prison. That will be the easiest money we ever made. Much easier than selling drugs. I won't have to bust my ass anymore."

In a separate trial, Ford's buddies pleaded guilty to the drug charges, and the judge gave them a sentence of three years.

In their celebration of the closing of the case at the Shangri-La, Zack said he thought it was terrible that the Ford family could make money from their crimes.

"This is America, Zack. There are always people around who are willing to make money from bad stuff. I doubt, however, if they will ever collect any money."

"Why is that?"

"An all-white family is going into prison as being hateful of Blacks and Mexicans will never get out alive. Prisoners have their own sense of justice. The Aryan nation will not able to protect them."

With these words, Zuma waved to the waiter to take their dinner orders. Pat had brought his new lady friend, and Zack was with a date. All six appeared to be enjoying each other's company with smiles and laughter together. Zuma lifted his glass and looked at Claudia.

"May you all be as lucky as I am to have found love. And may we all continue our friendships. True friends leave footprints in our heads and in our hearts, and neither my heart or head is heavy from your footprints."

He began humming and asked them to join in while he sang the words to "Lean on Me."

> Lean on me, when you're not strong
> And I'll be your friend
> I'll help you carry on
> For it won't be long
> 'Til I'm gonna need
> Somebody to lean on
> You just call on me brother, when you need a hand
> We all need somebody to lean on
> I just might have a problem that you'll understand
> We all need somebody to lean on

All the people at the table smiled. This was the Zuma they knew and loved.

www.ingramcontent.com/pod-product-compliance
Lightning Source LLC
Chambersburg PA
CBHW021452070526
44577CB00002B/379